For my parents and their journey
献给我历尽艰辛的父母
—J.L.

To Mom & Dad
—C.S.

Text copyright © 2019 by Julie Leung
Jacket art and interior illustrations copyright © 2019 by Chris Sasaki

All rights reserved. Published in the United States by Schwartz & Wade Books, an imprint of Random House Children's Books, a division of Penguin Random House LLC, New York.

Schwartz & Wade Books and the colophon are trademarks of Penguin Random House LLC.

Visit us on the Web! rhcbooks.com

Educators and librarians, for a variety of teaching tools, visit us at RHTeachersLibrarians.com

Library of Congress Cataloging-in-Publication Data is available upon request.
ISBN 978-1-5247-7187-4 (trade)
ISBN 978-1-5247-7188-1 (lib. bdg.)
ISBN 978-1-5247-7189-8 (ebook)

The text of this book is set in 7 Seconds.
The illustrations were rendered digitally.
Book design by Rachael Cole

MANUFACTURED IN CHINA
10 9 8 7 6 5 4 3 2 1
First Edition

PAPER SON

THE INSPIRING STORY OF *TYRUS WONG*, *IMMIGRANT AND ARTIST*

WRITTEN BY JULIE LEUNG ✦ ILLUSTRATED BY CHRIS SASAKI

schwartz & wade books • new york

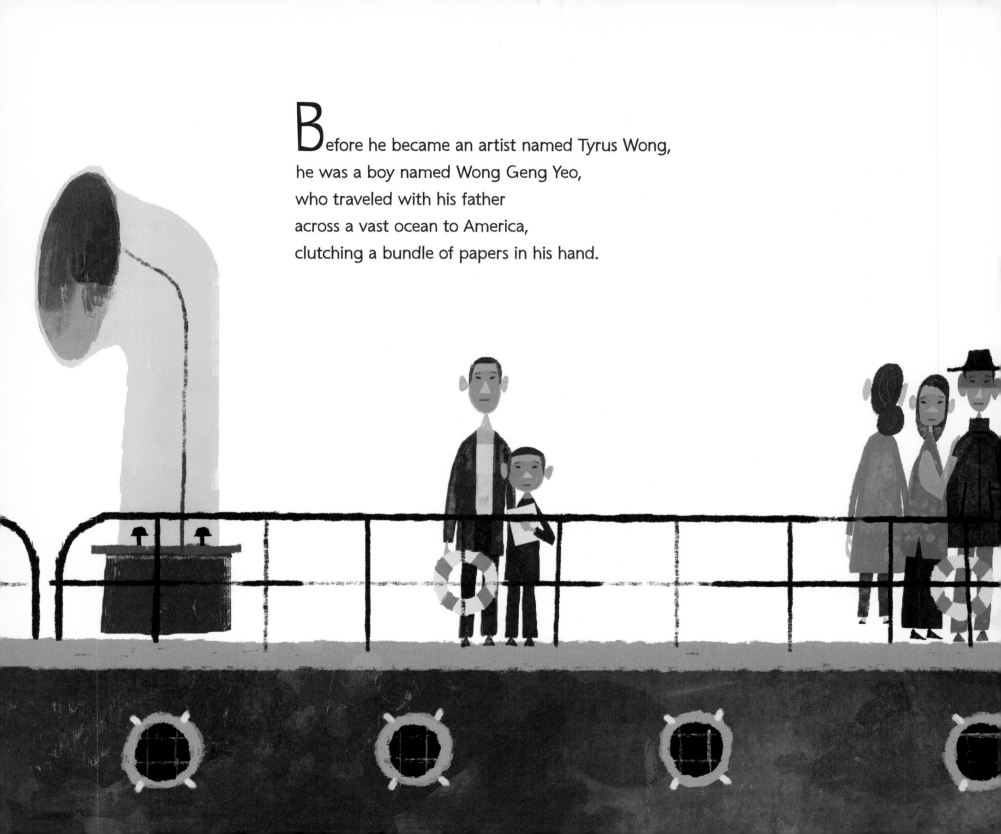

Before he became an artist named Tyrus Wong,
he was a boy named Wong Geng Yeo,
who traveled with his father
across a vast ocean to America,
clutching a bundle of papers in his hand.

The papers were not for drawing monkeys, which he loved to do.
They were papers describing the life of another Chinese boy,
whom Geng Yeo was pretending to be.
He had to memorize every word.

In 1919, Chinese immigrants were not allowed into the United States
unless they could prove they were citizens of high status:
a scholar, a merchant, a business owner,
or the child of such a citizen.
So the boy's father pretended to be a merchant named Look Git.
Wong Geng Yeo became his son, Look Tai Yow.
He was now a *zi jai,* a "paper son."

Every night, the boy studied the answers to exacting questions:
What are the names of the families who live in your village?
Who is the leader of your district?
How far is it to the next village?

"The immigration officials will ask me the same questions
and compare our answers to make sure you are my son," his father said.
"If they do not match, you will be sent back and never see Gum Saan."

Gum Saan means "Gold Mountain" in Cantonese.
That was what the Chinese called America,
because of the opportunities there.

"See?" his father would say, pointing to the horizon.
"Life in Gum Saan will be like a blank paper,
and we will decide how to mark it."
The boy followed his father's gaze
to where water met the sky.
Maybe he would spot a glimmer of Gold Mountain, too!

At last, they arrived at Angel Island.

His father, who had been in America before, cleared Immigration quickly.

But the boy was held back.

Scared and alone, Geng Yeo was taken to a wooden house filled with strangers.
There, he waited.

Days turned to weeks.
This new land was not what he expected.
The streets were not lined with gold.
The barracks were crowded and dirty.
He missed his father very much.

There was no drawing paper.
No ink. No paint.
He watched the sun move slowly across the sky,
always arching back toward the home he'd left behind.

Finally, Geng Yeo was brought in front of three men,
who bombarded him with questions:

"How many windows does your house have?"
"What direction does your village face?"
"Where did you go to school?"

The boy was nervous, but he remembered all his answers
from the coaching papers his father had given him.

He was released from Angel Island!
His father was waiting for him with arms outstretched.
"Now we must look for opportunities," he said.

At school in Sacramento,
Wong Geng Yeo was given a new name by his teachers,
a name that combined his real name
and his "paper" name:
Tai Yow was Americanized to Tyrus.
Tyrus Wong.

Tyrus did not like school.
He preferred sketching to science.
Doodles to diagrams.
Art to arithmetic.

354
x 71

Tyrus

Tyrus's father had been well educated in China,
but to be a Chinese immigrant was to be a servant, a laundryman, a waiter.
And to find these jobs, he often had to travel far, leaving Tyrus alone for months.

Still, his father believed life in America could be like a blank paper.
One day, he brought home a brush, and
made Tyrus practice Chinese calligraphy.
Because they could not afford ink and paper,
Tyrus wrote with water on old newspapers.
And after the paper dried, his father would say,
"One more time."

His father borrowed enough money
to send Tyrus to Otis Art Institute in Los Angeles.
Tyrus learned to paint and draw in the Western style,
smudging thick charcoal to form shadows
and mirroring the way light hits objects.

He also studied artwork from China's Song dynasty,
when watercolors and simple lines
communicated much by showing little.
The lushness of a flower could be felt
with gradual increases of color.
And mountains could loom in the distance
with a few jagged lines.

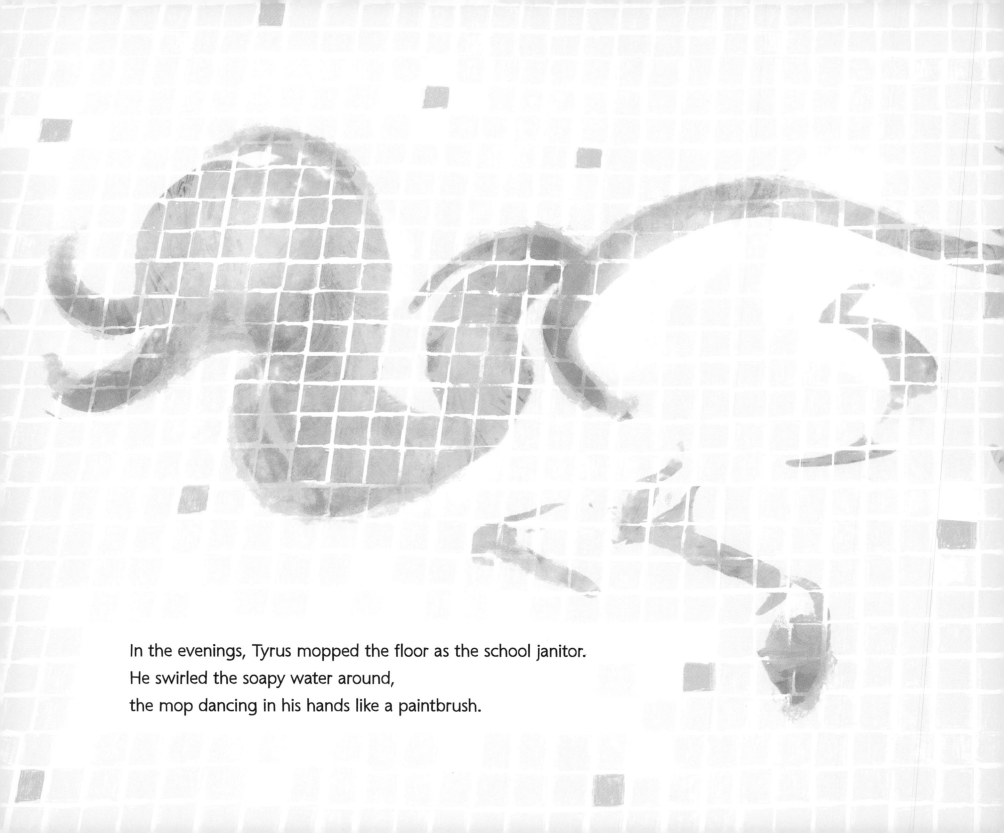

In the evenings, Tyrus mopped the floor as the school janitor.
He swirled the soapy water around,
the mop dancing in his hands like a paintbrush.

Tyrus graduated at the top of his class
and began working as an "in-betweener" at Walt Disney Studios.
In the early days of animation,
in-betweeners drew the frames "in between" a movie's key art—

the same scenes over and over,
with only small changes each time,
to create the feeling of movement.
The work was boring, and his eyes throbbed.

One day, Tyrus heard that Disney was making a movie called *Bambi*, about a young deer who must learn to survive without his mother. But the animators were having trouble creating the backgrounds.

Tyrus thought about the mother he had left behind in China,
and the father who always believed in him.
He thought about his style of painting—
one that combined East and West,
his past and his present.

Tyrus saw an opportunity.

He spent days painting landscapes.
Instead of drawing a forest scene leaf by leaf, tree by tree,
he created the *feeling* of woods and mountains
with sparse brushstrokes and soft watercolors.
Where other artists might use ten strokes of a brush,
he used five.

The result was breathtaking.

Walt Disney loved it.

He instructed his animators to follow Tyrus's style.

Bambi became a groundbreaking film.
Audiences and critics gushed about the art—
how it communicated so much by showing so little,
how you could almost smell the mossy green of the woods
and hear the rushing water of the brook.
But in the end, Tyrus was credited only as a background artist.

Walt Disney Studios fired Tyrus after an employee strike,
even though he did not participate.
It would be many years before the world saw Tyrus Wong
for the artist that he was.

But Tyrus never stopped painting,
and not just on paper.
Throughout his life, he would draw his art on
ceramics,
silk scarves,
murals,
menus.
Tyrus always found new ways to leave his mark.

As an old man, Tyrus discovered a love of kites:
Caterpillars and pandas.
Fish and butterflies.
He would tell people
he wanted to be looking up.
How else could one see Gold Mountain?

On sunny days, you could often find Tyrus Wong on the beach,
facing the ocean he crossed so long ago,
flying a large, colorful kite he'd made himself—
glimmering gold where water met the sky.

AUTHOR'S NOTE

When Tyrus Wong was just nine years old, he boarded the S.S. *China* with his father, seeking a brighter future in the United States. They immigrated during a time when the Chinese Exclusion Act—the first federal law designed to prevent an ethnic group from entering the country—was in full effect.

Tyrus's father knew that some exceptions were made—mainly for those of high social status or blood relatives of American citizens. To meet the criteria for entry, many immigrants assumed false identities. Forged papers that raised someone's status or falsely documented family ties to Americans were sold at a premium price, creating a black market for "paper" sons and daughters. From 1910 to 1940, over 170,000 Chinese were processed through Angel Island Immigration Station outside San Francisco Bay. An estimated 80 to 90 percent of them were paper sons and daughters, among them Tyrus Wong and his father.

From those humble beginnings, Tyrus would go on to graduate from Otis Art Institute with honors. In a time when most Chinese immigrants worked as manual laborers, this was no small feat.

In 1938, Tyrus got a job at Walt Disney Studios as a lowly in-betweener. When Disney began creating *Bambi,* Tyrus saw his chance and impressed Walt Disney with a series of magnificent landscape paintings. Promoted to inspirational sketch artist, he spent two years illustrating hundreds of scenes that would influence every part of the motion picture, down to the music and special effects. In the film's credits, he is listed merely as a background artist, despite his much larger role. His art direction, inspired by his knowledge of Chinese art, would in turn inspire a generation of American animators.

After Disney, Tyrus continued to work in Hollywood, illustrating scripts and storyboards for over two decades at Warner Bros. He also painted ceramics, holiday cards, magazine covers, scarves, and menus, and after he retired, he discovered a passion for kite building. In 2016, Tyrus passed away at the age of 106, after a lifetime of creating art.

I first learned about Tyrus Wong through his obituary in the *New York Times.* He was one of the preeminent Chinese American artists of our time, and yet, I had never heard of him. Growing up the only child of immigrants, I had very few picture books available to me about the accomplishments of fellow Chinese Americans—much less artists. I wanted to change that for future generations.

My own parents immigrated to the United States from a village just forty miles away from Taishan, where Tyrus and his father were from. In our families, I see the same resilience and ability to thrive in a new country that did not welcome them.

Despite the lack of recognition throughout his career, Tyrus Wong always found a way to express himself through art. His story reminds us that immigrants, wanted or not, leave an essential mark on the masterpiece that is this nation.

ILLUSTRATOR'S NOTE

Tyrus Wong has been a huge influence on me as an Asian American artist working in animation and illustration. I still remember being captivated by Tyrus's impressionistic work on *Bambi,* and how the atmospheric brushstrokes brought the sights, sounds, and smells of the forest to life in my childhood imagination.

Throughout his career, Tyrus drew inspiration from within. He remained honest to his craft and his Eastern heritage, paving the way for more widespread acceptance of Asian American artists. His story encourages me to never stop creating, and I hope his work is cherished for many future generations.

Tyrus (front right) pictured with schoolmates, 1923, *courtesy of the Tyrus Wong family*

Tyrus's immigration card, *courtesy of the Tyrus Wong family*

Tyrus posing for a Venus Watercolor Pencils advertisement, 1953, *courtesy of the Tyrus Wong family*

Tyrus with an owl kite, 2002, age 92, *courtesy of the Tyrus Wong family*

Tyrus and his family, 1957, *courtesy of the Tyrus Wong family*